PRAISE F

Ellery Littleton is observant, sensitive and very experienced in the deeper movements of the human psyche. In his poetry he captures poignant moments to which I relate with deep feeling. He writes of his own experiences, and in doing so, invites readers to respond from their own store of intimate personal memories.

The poems in *Travelling Light* reveal fundamental layers of meaning. Littleton teaches, not by instruction, but by sharing sharply rendered moments of universal meaning through the remarkably effective and vivid haiku form.

I recognize myself as I read these poems. I expect other readers will too if they are willing to take the time to become quiet and savour each one in turn.

JOCK MCKEEN, co-founder of The Haven

★★★

I am happy to write this glowing testimonial for Ellery Littleton's *Travelling Light*. The shadows it casts allow the deep insights to open my heart – such surprise is both magic and holy scripture, rooted down and blossoming through these poem seeds – lines you can breathe way inside, to carry you on.

JOHN FOX, author of *The Healing Art of Poem-Making*, The Institute for Poetic Medicine

Travelling Light

HAVEN HAIKU

Ellery Littleton

To Pam.

With affection

from Ellery.

June 2018.

ISBN 978-0-9697222-2-9

Designed and typeset by Toby Macklin
www.tobymacklin.com

To friends of The Haven everywhere ...

an idea
a place
a green house
for growing

FOREWORD

THE POEMS in this collection are truly "Haven Haiku" in that they are all in some way inspired by a place – The Haven on Gabriola Island, BC – and the experiences it offers.

The poems range from the obvious to the subtle – aspects of commonly-shared experiences at this remarkable place of learning and growth. My hope is that readers will recognize, in these mini-observations of Haven moments, something of their own experiences.

The Haven was established in 1983 by Bennet Wong and Jock McKeen, and has become, over the 30-some years of its existence, a striking example of what the "growth centre" of the 1960s has evolved into – a fully-rounded forum for the intimate, humanistic study of the self, and the self in relationship.

Moments of stark self-awareness or sudden understanding occur for most people who journey to The Haven in pursuit of self-awareness. These poems are intended to conjure up such moments; they are often humorous, poignant or tinged with deep feeling. One does not have to have been to The Haven to "get" the poems; many of them will ring bells of recognition for almost everybody.

The title of the book – *Travelling Light* – is drawn from one of the haiku in the series:

travelling light ...
just me and my life
at the workshop

This poem presents a lot of information in a short space, and has several levels of meaning – which is the essence of haiku. Haiku are the perfect form for capturing quick, intimate snapshots of times, places and moments of awareness. They are subtle and allusive, leaving lots of room for the imagination of the reader. Haiku aim to capture the universal in the moment, always with brevity and conciseness.

Haiku written in the traditional Japanese style are usually three lines long with 17 syllables, containing certain widely-understood symbolic and seasonal cultural references. The North American haiku, however, has evolved its own themes and forms, and has moved into direct expression of psychological observation. Haiku are still most often three lines long, but they can also be two or four, or even one line in length, and can contain anywhere from five to twenty syllables.

The intent of haiku, as in Zen, is "to show and

not tell." The form frees the writer from having to explain, and if done well, communicates with the reader in an instant. Because haiku are so short, readers may be tempted to rush through them. My suggestion is to read them slowly, allowing enough time for the meaning of each one to register.

There are a dozen or so poems towards the end of the book which were written specifically for The Haven's Chinese audience who attend programs every year. These poems – with translations in Mandarin – were crafted with the cultural background of these friends of The Haven in mind.

I want to thank:

Toby Macklin – program leader, faculty member, and graphic artist, for the elegant design of *Travelling Light*, and invaluable assistance in supervising its publication.

Rachel Davey, The Haven's Executive Director, for her whole-hearted support of the concept and publication of the book.

Cathy McNally, who told me she "loved the poems" after reading the first few, and encouraged me to go ahead.

Walter Cheng for his thoughtful translations into Chinese.

Bennet Wong and Jock McKeen, co-founders of The Haven, for their visionary leadership.

ELLERY LITTLETON,
Victoria, BC, September, 2015

Note. There are many fine collections of haiku, and books about the writing of haiku, on the market. If you were to read only one, I would suggest *The Haiku Apprentice: Memoirs of Writing Poetry in Japan* by Abigail Friedman, an engaging story of a literary and cultural voyage; a book for poets and non-poets.

TRAVELLING LIGHT

breathe ...
an island
a forest
a sunset
a dream

foolish, I know
but I do have this dream
about being myself

a relational world ...
loving compassion ...
integrity and respect ...
I want to live there

a relational world ...
loving compassion ...
integrity and respect ...
I want to live there

grow, transform and
connect ... plants do it
maybe I can too

there's something about
an island away from
the "real" world ...

... that allows me
to be here now ...
then be here again

talking of life
and death
in the afternoon

the forest!
the beach!
the ocean!!
when is dinner again?

there is nothing
so wise as
a circle

yin and yang
Ben and Jock
the circle is
unbroken

this program is for you
if you do not recognize
yourself in the mirror

seeking passion
purpose and meaning?
do I have a weekend
for you

let go of the past ...
live in the present ...
love myself?
let's not get carried away

sea lions barking
ravens croaking
someone singing
in the session room

remembering when
I first came alive
with Joann, Ernie and Ben

tonight I am feeling ...
and isn't that
amazing?

travelling light ...
just me and my life
at the workshop

my knees are knocking
but I have to take
the plunge

feeling small
in the group ...
better than not
feeling at all

Vesuvius!
a mountain I climbed
at Haven today

I told the story
beneath the story
which I had not
told before

I found my voice
the day I lost it
doing body work

I said what
I really felt
and nobody objected

when we argue
I'd like to be more
Italian

things would be better
if only you were
different ...

... or is it
the other way
round?

falling in love again
looking for the
big kahuna

distant and cool
he disdains my advances ...
still I desire him madly

shortest day of the year
longest day of my life
the day she left

to love somebody
who doesn't love me ...
what a horse's ass I am

(Old Japanese Proverb)
"the reverse side
has its reverse side" ...
why can't you see it
my way?

I do love you
but I want this
little safety zone
for now

at this moment
one koan has my
full attention ...
you

obsessing over you ...
even the naked dummy
in the boutique window
looks at me askance

the words were
the same as usual ...
then why do things
feel different today?

I try to hide my feelings
but he always asks
"what's the matter?"

I love you madly
but I really don't
like you

you remind me of my ex ...
I was attracted to you
immediately

if I leave this relationship
nothing will change ...
except my life!

you're the bull
and I'm the
china shop

it's not me ...
it's you who
always does this

I'm not listening ...
is that what
you're saying?

second husband stays
home while I attend
relationship workshops

you do give me
plenty of opportunities
to hurt myself

we've analyzed this
to death ...
bugger off!

I can't see myself
except as a shadow
or a reflection

dialogue with my body ...
boy did I get
an earful

dialogue with the little
woman ... the little
woman inside me

heal the past
heal the present
change the story

in the seeing
comes the
moving

if you're doing it
you're digging it
whatever it is

despite my procrastinations
I am still on the path
of awareness

if I punish myself
often enough
I won't have to change

I always knew
it wouldn't last
but ignored the past
and did it all over again

through tears
I check myself
in the mirror

I've fallen off the wagon
again ... but the wagon's
still waiting for me

the person within
the person is waiting
to hear from you

déjà vu ... I'm black
and blue ... but I'm
coming alive today

I love your disguise …
will you be taking it off
for the party?

not just talking the talk
but walking the walk
for a change

walking the walk
all the way
to the point
of no return

through a glass darkly
into the future ...
here I go again

it was a time when ...
the song ended
the bell rang
I had to do something

it was a time when
I had to choose
and here is where
I ended up

I did not ask
but still you
gave me gifts

did I say "thank-you?"
I never could
but now I am

fearful hopeful
freaked-out
and fucked-up ...
I'm here

noticing it
moving on
not judging myself
so harshly

I did not hurt
myself once
today …

… although several
golden opportunities
came up

defensive, narcissistic
arrogant, afraid
of being seen

my unconscious
gives me a gift ...
a dream

I wonder why
the Creator decided
that dreams should be
in code?

Fellini has been
directing my dreams
of late

writing in my journal ...
sorting things out
with myself

my wise companion
waits patiently for me
in my journal

my guru ...
my guide ...
my journal

in my journal
I give myself
the best advice

I wore my shame
like a shawl
made of silk
insinuations

what does my body
language say
about me?

your body speaks
with a distinctly
European accent

I am afraid of what
this day may bring ...
but so happy
to be here

I hate myself
when I hate
myself

when I listen
carefully to myself
I am myself
at my best

after the workshop
I said to myself
"if I can do that
I can do anything"

at the cemetery today
visiting the ancestors
visiting myself

just because
they're dead
doesn't mean
they don't need
to be loved

you can't blame
mom and dad
forever

I wonder if they know
that I have long since
forgiven them

my relationship
with my father
improved dramatically
after he died

I saw my mother
in the mirror
this morning

sitting by their graves
I ask them to be patient ...
I will be along soon

Canadian standoff ...
my parents'
marriage

body language ...
each family
has its own

remembering
who they were ...
the essence of
who I am

the family portrait ...
and there I am
right in the middle

dialogue with my father ...
warmer softer
still a bit prickly

dialogue with my
mother ...
she loves me
and I feel it ...

... but she would
still like me
to do something
with my hair

I am who they were
except for the part
that is just me

in letting them go
I welcome
them in

life's an illusion ...
such a painful
illusion sometimes!

"is that so?"
is often all that
needs to be said

as far as I can see
it's all about me
but you seem to think
it isn't

forgive me
if I stop thinking
once in a while

like Ama the pearl diver
I am swimming through
deep waters

lonely afternoon ...
leafing through
The Joy of Sex

who's that knocking
at my heart?
shadow ...

... shadow who
knows both good
and evil lurk within

even if you don't
show me yours
I want to show
you mine

my friend won't join me
at the workshop today ...
it's all bullshit anyway
he says ...

... but he's wrong
it's elephant shit
and he'll always be
my friend

dinner on the deck
for one ... just me
and the sea
and the eagles

how can I be
here now
when I wasn't
there then?

when I worry
it's always the
worst-case scenario ...

... when I get there
it usually
isn't

stepping stones ...
each one says
"after that I was
never the same"

I'll believe
everything
you tell me ...
at least once

you can't
or you won't?
they're not
the same

without the shadow
the light means
nothing

they say you can't go back
again ... but I do go back again
I must go back again ...

... but having said that
I know it's better
to be here now

CHINESE HAIKU

I am at home
in this place
far away
from home

这里
如同回家一般
虽然
身在遥远的他乡

pausing to pray
in the garden ...
I say goodbye to
my revered friend

(in memory of Bennet Wong)

在花园里
停下来祈祷…
我向我敬重的朋友
道别

（纪念黄焕祥）

in the group
a new sensation ...
feeling alone

置身于团体中
一种全新的感觉···
有些孤独

listening openly
speaking openly
no bosses here

敞开地聆听
敞开地分享
没人需要服从谁

it's okay they say
falling in love
but I'm not sure
it's okay for me

他们可以分享说
自己恋爱了
但我不确定
我是不是一样可以

my family, my work
my country, myself ...
who comes first?

我的家庭，我的工作
我的国家，我自己…
哪个排第一？

arranged marriage
arranged job
arranged life ...

... but I refuse
to be arranged
and choose to be
myself

被安排的婚姻
被安排的工作
被安排的生活…

…但我拒绝
被安排
我选择
做自己

beautiful song
touches my heart
and I remember you

动人的歌曲
触碰我的心灵
我记起了你

in this green
and peaceful place
I hardly miss
my busy life

在这个充满绿色
安静祥和的地方
我几乎忘记了
繁忙的生活

taking time to find out
who I am and what
I want to do

慢下来，去探寻
我是谁
我想要做什么

singing favorite songs
after dinner with the group
I am amazingly happy

晚饭后和大家一起
唱我最喜欢的歌谣
我无比开心

to be free ... to choose ...
to refuse ... to be myself ...
the impossible dream?

要自由…要选择…
要说不…要做自己…
是虚幻的梦吗?

ABOUT THE AUTHOR

Ellery Littleton lives in Victoria, BC, Canada. He has been a Haven faculty member for 25 years, offering journal- and poetry-writing workshops.

His previous books include:

Old Rocks, New Streams: 64 Poems from The I Ching
Time Crimes (a novel)
Riverwalk: A Poem A Day for A year
Hummingbird Tattoo (erotic haiku)

All are available at The Haven store, or directly from the author: littleton@shaw.ca

The Haven
240 Davis Road
Gabriola Island, BC
VOR 1X1
Canada

Tel. 1 800 222 9211
info@haven.ca
www.haven.ca